Today's Superstars

Entertainment

The Olsen Twins

by Jacqueline Laks Gorman

Gareth Stevens
Publishing

Please visit our web site at: www.garethstevens.com
For a free color catalog describing Gareth Stevens Publishing's
list of high-quality books, call 1-800-542-2595 (USA)
or 1-800-387-3178 (Canada).

Library of Congress Cataloging-in-Publication Data

Gorman, Jacqueline Laks, 1955-
　　The Olsen Twins / by Jacqueline Laks Gorman.
　　　　p. cm. — (Today's superstars. Entertainment)
　　Includes bibliographical references and index.
　　ISBN: 978-0-8368-8199-8 (lib. bdg.)
　　1. Olsen, Ashley, 1986—Juvenile literature. 2. Olsen, Mary-Kate,
1986—Juvenile literature. 3. Actors—United States—Biography—
Juvenile literature. I. Title.
PN2287.O36G67　　2008
792.02'8092273—dc22
　　[B]　　　　　　　　　　　　　　　　　　2007005189

This edition first published in 2008 by
Gareth Stevens Publishing
A Weekly Reader® Company
1 Reader's Digest Road
Pleasantville, NY 10570-7000 USA

Copyright © 2008 by Gareth Stevens, Inc.

Editor: Gini Holland
Art direction and design: Tammy West
Picture research: Diane Laska-Swanke
Production: Jessica Yanke

Photo credits: Cover, © George Pimentel/WireImage.com; p. 5 © Paul McConnell/Getty Images; p. 7 © Eric Ryan/Getty Images; pp. 9, 10, 11 © Warner Brothers/courtesy Everett Collection; p. 13 © Universal/courtesy Everett Collection; p. 15 The Everett Collection; p. 16 © Online USA/Getty Images; pp. 18, 25, 26 © AP Images; p. 20 © NBC/courtesy Everett Collection; p. 22 © Mark Mainz/Getty Images; p. 28 © Jamie McCarthy/WireImage.com

All rights reserved. No part of this book may be reproduced, stored in a retrieval system, or transmitted in any form or by any means, electronic, mechanical, photocopying, recording, or otherwise, without the prior written permission of the copyright holder.

Printed in the United States of America

1 2 3 4 5 6 7 8 9 11 10 09 08 07

Contents

Chapter 1 Designing Stars 4

Chapter 2 Out of the Ordinary 8

Chapter 3 Building an Empire 14

Chapter 4 Growing Pains 19

Chapter 5 Taking Control 24

Time Line 29

Glossary 30

To Find Out More 31

Index 32

Chapter 1: Designing Stars

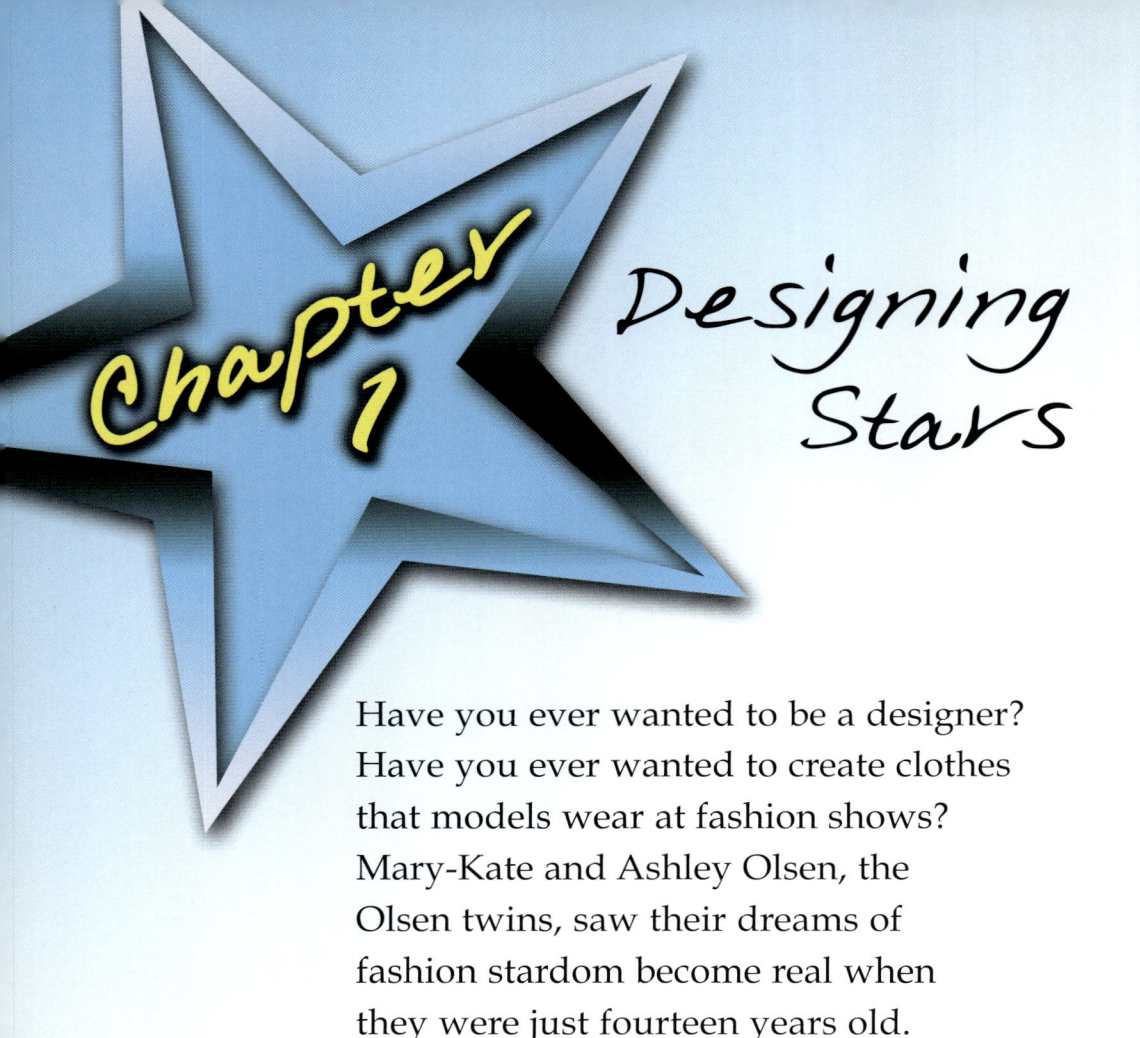

Have you ever wanted to be a designer? Have you ever wanted to create clothes that models wear at fashion shows? Mary-Kate and Ashley Olsen, the Olsen twins, saw their dreams of fashion stardom become real when they were just fourteen years old.

Mary-Kate and Ashley were already TV stars. They already had a successful company that produced the books and videos they starred in. The sisters were famous, so they had a lot of influence on kids their age. Starting their own clothing line gave them even more success and influence. Their famous faces and new designs made them powerful forces in the fashion world.

Mary-Kate and Ashley attended a fashion show of their clothes in Sydney, Australia, in February 2006. The Olsens' clothing line is sold around the world.

A Line of Their Own

In January 2001, the mary-kateandashley clothing line went on sale at stores across the United States. The Olsen twins had been interested in fashion for a long time. At age ten, they had begun working with a designer to help choose the clothes they wore in their videos. By the time they were twelve, the twins wanted more sophisticated clothes than stores were selling for girls their

Fact File

Mary-Kate and Ashley tell the designers of their clothing line what the clothes should look like. "We're firm about what kinds of products we'll put our names on," Mary-Kate says. "It doesn't make sense to put out something we don't like."

5

age. To please their fashion sense, their own designer bought adult clothes and fixed them so they fit the twins.

Fans liked the way Mary-Kate and Ashley dressed. Many wanted to dress like the famous twins, and soon, the mary-kateandashley brand was born. The line was introduced with an exciting fashion show and party in Hollywood, which were shown on TV. The clothes — which included jeans, tops, shoes, and pajamas — were made for girls ages six to eleven years old. The larger sizes were for a new market of girls, the "tween" market.

The brand did not stop with clothes. Soon, fans could buy all sorts of Olsen products, including cosmetics, toothpaste, and sheets. Mary-Kate and Ashley had moved well beyond TV and videos. They now ran a business empire. They now influenced the lives of teen and tween girls in many ways — and they haven't stopped yet.

Fact File

By 2003, mary-kateandashley clothes were being sold around the world.

Tweens

Tweens are preteens, children between the ages of eight and twelve. The tween market developed in the 1990s. Companies realized that these children were not teenagers yet, but tweens often liked the teenage look. Many companies began making products just for the tween market, including Mary-Kate and Ashley's company. "My sister and I started the whole tween empire," Ashley once said.

Many tweens like to follow the latest fads, act grown up, and dress in sophisticated clothes. They have made the mary-kateandashley clothes and other products very popular.

Chapter 2
Out of the Ordinary

Mary-Kate and Ashley have been famous since they were babies. The girls' father, Dave, was a businessman. Their mother, Jarnette, used to be a ballet dancer. The girls' brother, Trent, was two years older than the twins when they were born. When they were seven months old, the twins' mother took them to a modeling agency. "I just thought it might be fun," Jarnette later said. "It was a way to get out of the house and do something a little out of the ordinary."

Full House

The people at the agency sent the girls to try out for a new television show, a comedy

Fact File

Ashley's middle name is Fuller, which is her mother's maiden name. Mary-Kate does not have a middle name.

Full House starred Bob Saget (*holding Mary-Kate*) as Danny Tanner. He raises his daughters with the help of his brother-in-law and best friend.

called *Full House*. The part was for a baby named Michelle. In California, the law sets a limit on the number of hours a child actor or actress can work. Because of this rule, the producers of *Full House* wanted twins to share the part of baby Michelle.

The executive producer had already picked another set of twins to play Michelle. He changed his mind and gave the part to Mary-Kate and Ashley. "I just thought they were so unique," he said. "They had these big, expressive eyes. They were friendly, they listened when you spoke to them, and they would really respond to you!"

Fact File

At first, the producers of *Full House* did not want people to know that more than one actress played Michelle. The credits at first said "Mary Kate Ashley Olsen," as if the part were played by one person.

9

In *Full House*, Michelle's older sisters were played by Jodie Sweetin (*left*) and Candace Cameron (*right*). The twins have stayed in touch with their *Full House* family.

Fact File

Ashley is right-handed and Mary-Kate is left-handed. On *Full House*, the Michelle character uses both her right and left hands when she writes, eats, and so on.

Growing Up in Public

Full House appeared on TV for the first time on September 22, 1987. The show was about Danny Tanner and his family. Danny's wife had just died in a car accident, and he needed help raising his three daughters — D.J., Stephanie, and little Michelle. To help him out, Danny's brother-in-law and best friend move in.

Full House was an instant hit. Families got together in front of their television sets each week to see what the Tanner girls would do next. The household was warm and loving. Each episode ended happily.

Michelle was one of the most popular characters. When the Olsen twins began to talk, their Michelle character began to say funny things, such as "You got it, dude" and "No way, José." As the twins got older, their different personalities showed. Mary-Kate acted in the funny,

Twins

Twins happen when a mother gives birth to two children from the same pregnancy. In the United States, twins happen in about one out of eighty-seven pregnancies. Twins can be identical or fraternal. Identical twins, who are more rare, are always the same sex and look alike. Fraternal twins may be different sexes. They may look alike or look different, just like any brothers and sisters. Even though Mary-Kate and Ashley look very much alike, they are fraternal twins. The Olsens are just one pair of famous twins. Others include the actresses Tia and Tamera Mowry, the football players Ronde and Tiki Barber, and Barbara and Jenna Bush, the daughters of President George W. Bush.

The producers of *Full House* needed twins to share the role of Michelle. One reason Mary-Kate and Ashley were chosen was because they were the only twins who did not cry at the audition.

Fact File

Ashley is two minutes older than Mary-Kate.

emotional scenes. Ashley acted in the serious, sensitive scenes.

A Normal Life
When the twins were three years old, their parents had another baby. They named her Elizabeth, but everyone called her Lizzie.

A man named Robert Thorne became the girls' manager when they were four-and-one half years old. He helped the twins get involved in other projects. In 1992, the girls released their first record, called *Brother for Sale*. They also appeared in a TV movie called *To Grandmother's House We Go*. They played six-year-old twins who run away from home to give their mother some time off.

In their real life, the twins started school when they were old enough. Even though Mary-Kate and Ashley were TV stars, their parents tried to make the Olsen house and family as normal as possible. When *Full House* was filming, they had a private tutor on the set. When *Full House* was not filming, they went to a private school for regular classes. They were popular actresses, but they were kids, too.

Famous Child Stars

Child stars are children who are successful actors or actresses. Some stop acting when they get older, while others keep acting. Shirley Temple (1928-) was one of the most popular child stars of all time. She began singing and dancing in movies when she was only three years old, but she stopped acting when she got older. She became an ambassador to Ghana and Czechoslovakia. Judy Garland (1922-1969) sang on stage and radio from the time she was two and a half. She started appearing in movies when she was fourteen, and she starred in the film *The Wizard of Oz* when she was only seventeen. As an adult, she appeared in many concerts and was considered one of the greatest singers of all time.

Many current stars began their careers as children. Drew Barrymore starred in *E.T. the Extra-Terrestrial* when she was only seven. Jodie Foster appeared in her first commercial when she was a baby. She has won two Oscars. Ron Howard was in his first movie as a toddler. He became a popular TV child star as Opie on the *Andy Griffith Show*. He then became a teen TV star on *Happy Days*. He is now a successful director and won an Oscar as Best Director in 2002.

Drew Barrymore is now a successful movie star. When she was only seven, she appeared in the movie *E.T. the Extra-Terrestrial*, one of the most popular films of all time.

Chapter 3: Building an Empire

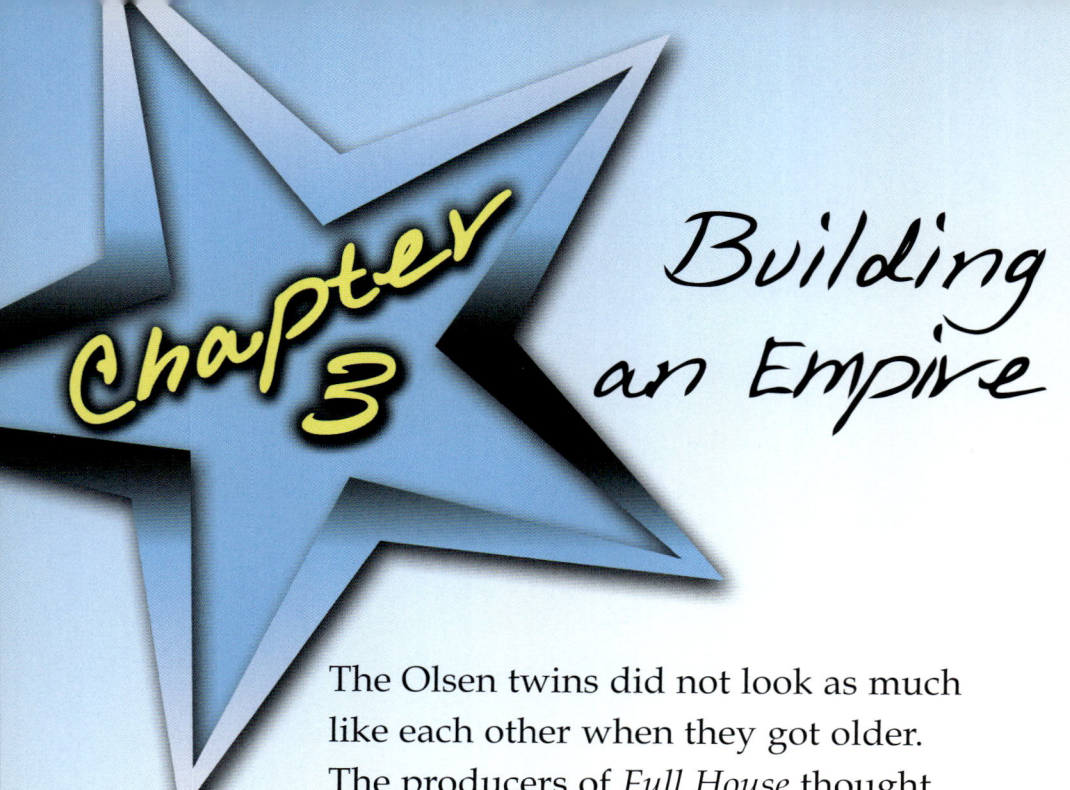

The Olsen twins did not look as much like each other when they got older. The producers of *Full House* thought about choosing just one of the girls to play Michelle. The twins were so popular, though, that the idea was dropped.

In 1993, Mary-Kate and Ashley and their manager started a company called Dualstar to produce projects for the twins. The twins took an active role in the company. They were the youngest producers in entertainment history!

That year, the twins starred in a TV movie called *Double, Double, Toil and Trouble*. They also released an album and a music video. In 1994, they were in another TV movie, *How the West Was Fun*. The twins' first video series,

The video series *The Adventures of Mary-Kate and Ashley* led to a popular series of books based on the twins' detective characters.

The Adventures of Mary-Kate and Ashley, also began in 1994. The girls played detectives, called the Trenchcoat Twins, whose motto was "will solve any crime by dinner time."

Changes

Full House went off the air in 1995. Mary-Kate and Ashley faced other changes, too. About the same time, their parents got a divorce. In 1996, their father married again. Within a few years, Mary-Kate and Ashley had a half-sister, Taylor, and a half-brother, Jake.

Some people thought that the end of *Full House* meant the end of the twins' career. If anything, the twins were now even busier. They

Fact File

The twins appeared on screen together in four episodes of *Full House*. In one episode, Ashley played Michelle while Mary-Kate, wearing a black wig, played a cousin visiting from Greece. In the final episode of the series, Michelle falls off a horse and forgets who she is. Michelle (played by one twin) talks to her "memory" (played by the other twin), until she remembers everything.

Mattel introduced this line of dolls, modeled after the Olsen twins, in 2000.

worked harder, got involved in more projects, and were more popular than ever.

It Takes Two, the twins' first movie, came out in 1995. After that, the girls were busy appearing in videos and on TV. Their second video series, *You're Invited to Mary-Kate & Ashley's*, began in 1995. In each video, the girls invited the viewer to a party. Each party had a theme, such as a sleepover or a Hawaiian beach party. They had two TV series, *Two of a Kind* in 1998 through 1999 and *So Little Time* in 2001 through 2002. In

Fact File

Mary-Kate remembers being on *Full House* fondly. "We grew up around all the people on *Full House*," she said. "That's what made it so much fun for us to go to work each day. We didn't do it because we had to. We did it because we loved it."

Exotic Places

Mary-Kate and Ashley liked to travel, so they chose interesting places for their videos. They also chose interesting activities to do. Some of the episodes of *The Adventures of Mary-Kate & Ashley* were set at Sea World in Florida, on a volcano, and on a naval destroyer. To make the video *The Case of the U.S. Space Camp Mission*, the girls went to an actual space camp with their father and their brother Trent. In the video *You're Invited to Mary-Kate and Ashley's Ballet Party*, they met members of the New York City Ballet. The girls also traveled to wonderful cities such as Paris, Rome, and London to film their videos.

2001, they also did the voices for an animated show, *Mary-Kate and Ashley in ACTION!*, about teenage secret agents. The twins were executive producers on their projects. They picked the locations, helped come up with the stories, and were involved in choosing the casts.

Fans watched the shows and bought all the videos. They also played with Olsen fashion dolls, made by Mattel, and Olsen video games. They read Olsen books. Some were based on the girls' videos and TV series, while others were new stories. When the mary-kateandashley brand came out in 2001, many fans

Fact File

Before the twins reached the age of ten, they were the youngest self-made millionaires in U.S. history!

Mary-Kate (*left*) and Ashley (*right*) appeared at a convention in 2000 to promote their video games. The games were based on their popular books and videos.

began to wear Olsen clothes. They bought Olsen accessories, and many even brushed their teeth with Olsen brand toothpaste.

Being Teenagers
Even though they were rich and famous, Mary-Kate and Ashley said they led normal lives. "Most of the time we do what every other teen does," Mary-Kate said. "We go to school, hang out with our friends, and go out on dates," Ashley said. Both girls liked shopping, going to the movies, and going to the beach. Mary-Kate loved horseback riding, while Ashley liked to dance and play golf.

Still, the Olsens were not regular teenagers. On their sixteenth birthdays in 2002, each girl got her own luxury SUV. Before their seventeenth birthdays in 2003, it was reported that each twin was worth $150 million.

Chapter 4

Growing Pains

In April 2004, Mary-Kate and Ashley got a star on the Hollywood Walk of Fame. They were the youngest people ever to get this honor. Soon after, the girls graduated from Campbell Hall, a private high school. They could not attend the prom because they were hosting the TV show *Saturday Night Live*. To make up for that, the cast threw a prom for them at the beginning of the show.

Troubling Times

Until this time, the girls had been successful at everything they did. Fans and critics, however, did not like their next movie, the romantic comedy

Fact File

When the girls were younger, they were asked if they wanted to go to different colleges. "I don't think so," Mary-Kate said. "Going to college is such an important time in your life. You know, a new place, new people, new experiences. I don't think I could be without my sister, too."

19

Instead of going to their real prom, Ashley danced with Jimmy Fallon (*left*) while Mary-Kate danced with Will Forte (*right*) on *Saturday Night Live* in May 2004.

New York Minute. The Olsens had hoped the movie would be the beginning of their adult acting careers.

Something more upsetting happened next. Mary-Kate was much too thin. She had an eating disorder. In June 2004, she entered a clinic for treatment. Mary-Kate was at the clinic for six weeks. Thanks to treatment, she gained five to seven pounds there. After she left the clinic, she continued to get help. She worked with therapists, nutritionists, and eating coaches.

New York, New York

In September 2004, the Olsens entered New York University (NYU) in New York City. They were enrolled in a part of NYU where

Eating Disorders

Eating disorders are a dangerous problem faced by many young people. The most common types are anorexia and bulimia. People with anorexia think they are overweight even when they are very, very thin. They are afraid of gaining weight, so they stop eating. People who have bulimia eat a lot in a short time, and then they try to make themselves vomit. Eating disorders usually develop in teenagers or young adults. They are more common in girls and women. These conditions are very dangerous. They can hurt the heart and other parts of the body. More than 10 percent of people with anorexia die from starvation, heart disease, or suicide.

Many people with anorexia need to go to the hospital to help them gain weight and think better about their bodies. Treatment may take years. Experts say there is too much pressure put on young people to want to be thin. Many say that extra-thin actresses and models on TV, in movies, and in magazines can make thin bodies look glamorous when, in fact, they are just unhealthy.

students design their own courses of study. Both girls took writing classes. In addition, Mary-Kate took photography. She worked with a famous photographer. Ashley took Italian. She also worked with a designer.

Being Famous, Being Followed

The twins were busy in New York.

Fact File

In late 2004, the Olsens signed a petition to help the women who make mary-kateandashley clothes. The women work in factories in Bangladesh. The petition asked Wal-Mart to give the workers paid maternity leave, which is several months off with pay, when they have babies.

In addition to going to school, they often went shopping. Like most college students, they went to restaurants and to dance clubs. But they needed more protection than normal college students. Bodyguards often went with them.

Like many famous people, the girls did not have much privacy. Whenever they went out, it seemed that reporters and photographers followed them. Newspapers and magazines printed pictures and stories about the twins. They reported about what the girls did and about their boyfriends.

The Olsens have had some interesting boyfriends. Ashley dated Matt Kaplan, a Columbia student and football player, for three years until they broke up in mid-2004. She also dated a nightclub owner

Mary-Kate and Ashley greet fans at the New York premiere of their film *New York Minute* in May 2004.

Famous People and Privacy

Famous people often have to give up some of their privacy. They know that photographers are always waiting to take pictures of them and their friends. The pictures are printed in newspapers and magazines. One of the most popular magazines in the United States, *People* began in 1974. It features stories about famous people. Another popular publication is the *National Enquirer*, which prints shocking pictures and stories about famous people. The *National Enquirer* pays photographers a lot of money for pictures that show stars looking bad or doing bad things. Some people think there should be laws stopping photographers from invading the privacy of famous people. Other people say that the photographers are just taking pictures of stars that the public wants to see. They also say that the photographers are actually helping the stars, because the stars need to be in the spotlight to help their careers.

and an executive at a clothing company. Mary-Kate dated the son of a film producer. She also dated Stavros Niarchos II, the heir to a fortune.

The Olsens are used to being famous and being watched all the time. For them, this is the price of success. "We've been working since we were born, basically," Mary-Kate said, "and we grew up with it. I love my work and I'm willing to live with both the benefits and the downside. As long as I'm doing what makes me happy, that's all that really matters."

Chapter 5
Taking Control

Mary-Kate and Ashley are now in full control of their company, Dualstar. Part of the company had belonged to their manager and later partner, Robert Thorne. In January 2005, the twins bought that part. They hired new people to help run the company. Dualstar once concentrated on making and selling videos, books, CDs, and dolls. Now, the company concentrates on clothing, cosmetics, fashion accessories, and products for the home.

The Olsens also expanded their Web site (mary-kateandashley.com). The site gives information and advice on health, beauty, fashion, and design. It also has a "Thought for the Day."

The twins take an active role in developing their clothing line. Here, Mary-Kate (*left*) and Ashley (*right*) look over some of the items in their 2005 line.

More than three thousand stores around the United States now sell mary-kateandashley clothes. They are sold in more than five thousand stores in other countries, too. In 2006, Mary-Kate and Ashley started a brand for boys. Called Sprouse Bros, it features the twins Dylan and Cole Sprouse.

Leading Ladies of Fashion

From the time the mary-kateandashley clothing line began in 2001, designers and fashion writers have praised the twins for their outstanding sense of style. The Olsens have set new fashion trends.

Fact File

Ashley appeared on the cover of *Harper's Bazaar* magazine in July 2005. It was the first time she ever appeared in a magazine without her sister.

25

The twins appeared in a fashion show for the high-fashion line Badgley Mischka in 2006. Here, they meet backstage with the designers (*from left*): Mark Badgley, Ashley, Mary-Kate, and James Mischka.

Time magazine named the ten most powerful women in fashion in 2004. Mary-Kate and Ashley were listed at number four! *Time* called them "the queens of all things teen." The twins plan to move beyond tweens and teens with a new high-fashion line called The Row. These clothes will be more sophisticated and expensive than those in their mary-kateandashley clothing line, which are for average-income buyers.

The twins have already been part of the high-fashion world. In April 2006, they appeared in ads for a design company called Badgley Mischka. The designers said, "Ashley and Mary-Kate have grown up to become America's young style icons. They have an amazing sense of fashion. . . ."

Mary-Kate's Special Style

Newspapers and magazines often show pictures of Mary-Kate dashing around New York or Los Angeles. She dresses in original clothes. She likes to wear boots, floppy hats, loose sweaters, long, full skirts, and big sunglasses. Other young women have copied Mary-Kate's style. The look can even be seen in fashion shows. Mary-Kate is such a trendsetter that a long article in the *New York Times* was called "Mary-Kate, Fashion Star." The magazine *Teen Vogue* called her "an honest-to-goodness style icon."

At the end of 2006, Mary-Kate and Ashley appeared on separate covers of *Teen Vogue*. The magazine talked about each girl's special style. Mary-Kate's style is more off-beat, while Ashley's style is more classic.

Going It Alone

Mary-Kate and Ashley have almost always been together. Now, they are doing more things on their own. In the fall of 2005, Mary-Kate settled in Los Angeles so she could concentrate on business. Ashley remained in school in New York.

Mary-Kate also took on a small acting role without her sister in the movie *Factory Girl*.

Fact File

When the Olsens appeared in ads for the design company Badgley Mischka, it was the first time they ever promoted a brand that was not their own.

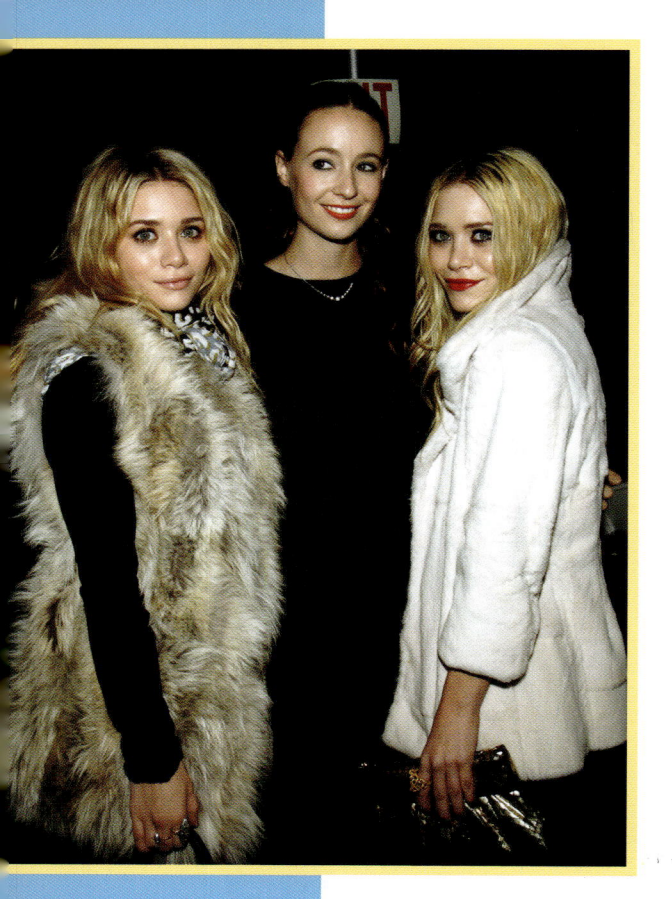

To keep up with the latest designs, the twins attended "Fashion Week" in New York City in February 2007.

Mary-Kate liked being just an actress again — not the person running the show.

Looking Forward
What does the future hold for the Olsen twins? Dualstar plans to seek out and develop new stars in the areas of fashion and entertainment. Mary-Kate and Ashley will certainly be involved in that. They will use their taste and talent to spot trends and figure out what the public wants.

Whatever Mary-Kate and Ashley do, they will be true to themselves. "What sets us apart from everyone else," Ashley said, "is that we have always stayed true to ourselves. . . . We have always just done things and created products that we want our name on. We have stayed loyal to ourselves and our fans, and that is, I think, what people admire."

Time Line

1986 — Ashley Fuller Olsen and Mary-Kate Olsen are born on June 13 in Sherman Oaks, California.

1987 — Begin appearing in the TV show *Full House*, which runs until 1995.

1992 — Release their first record, *Brother for Sale*, and appear in the TV movie *To Grandmother's House We Go*.

1993 — Start the company Dualstar; star in the TV movie *Double, Double, Toil and Trouble*.

1994 — Star in the TV movie *How the West Was Fun* and first video series, *The Adventures of Mary-Kate and Ashley*.

1995 — Appear in first movie, *It Takes Two*, and second video series, *You're Invited to Mary-Kate & Ashley's*.

2001 — Introduce mary-kateandashley clothing.

2004 — Graduate from high school and enter New York University.

2005 — Gain full control of Dualstar; Mary-Kate takes a leave of absence from NYU.

2006 — Appear on separate covers of *Teen Vogue*; Mary-Kate appears in the film *Factory Girl*.

Glossary

accessory — something that goes with your clothes, such as a scarf or jewelry, to make the entire outfit look better.
brand — the company name of a product.
credibility — believability.
critic — a person who makes a living by giving opinions about music, movies, art, or books.
designer — someone who creates the original pattern or design for something, especially clothes.
fashion — a style of clothing that is popular.
icon — a famous person who is admired for a particular activity.
market — a special group of customers for a particular type of goods.
nutritionist — someone who is a specialist in nutrition, the study of eating foods to stay healthy.
petition — a letter that many people sign to demand a specific action from people in power.
producer — someone in charge of the making of a movie, television program, play, or recording.
sophisticated — having a lot of experience or knowledge about the world.
therapist — someone who helps treat an illness or condition without using drugs or surgery.
tutor — a teacher who gives private lessons to a student or small group of students.
tween — a preteen, generally between the ages of eight and twelve.

To Find Out More

Books

Mary-Kate and Ashley Olsen. People in the News (series). Terri Dougherty (Lucent Books).

Mary-Kate and Ashley Olsen. Star Files (series). Stephanie Fitzgerald (Raintree).

Our Story: Mary-Kate and Ashley Olsen's Official Biography. Mary-Kate Olsen and Ashley Olsen, as told to Damon Romine (HarperEntertainment)

Videos

Full House (Seasons 1 to 6) (Warner Home Video) not rated

New York Minute (Warner Home Video) PG

You're Invited to Mary-Kate & Ashley's Greatest Parties (Warner Home Video)

Web Sites

Full House
www.tv.com/full-house/show/1026/summary.html
All about *Full House*, with information on the stars

Mary-Kate and Ashley on the Web
mary-kateandashley.com
The Olsen twins' official site, including an online diary, advice, and information about their products

Publisher's note to educators and parents: Our editors have carefully reviewed these Web sites to ensure that they are suitable for children. Many Web sites change frequently, however, and we cannot guarantee that a site's future contents will continue to meet our high standards of quality and educational value. Be advised that children should be closely supervised whenever they access the Internet.

Index

Adventures of Mary-Kate and Ashley, The 15, 17
Badgley Mischka 26, 27
books 15, 17
boyfriends 22–23
Brother for Sale 12
child stars 13
Double, Double, Toil and Trouble 14
Dualstar 14, 24, 28
eating disorders 20, 21
Factory Girl 27
fashion design 4, 5, 26, 28
fashion style 25, 26, 27
Full House 9, 10, 11, 12, 14, 15, 16

How the West Was Fun 14
It Takes Two 16
Mary-Kate and Ashley in ACTION! 17
mary-kateandashley 5, 6, 7, 17, 21, 24, 25
National Enquirer 23
New York City 20, 21, 22, 28
New York Minute 20, 22
New York University 20
Olsen, Dave 8, 15, 17
Olsen, Elizabeth 12
Olsen, Jarnette 8
Olsen, Trent 8, 17
People magazine 23
privacy 22, 23

Saturday Night Live 19, 20
school 12, 19, 20, 21, 22, 27
So Little Time 16
Sprouse brothers 25
Tanner, Michelle (TV character) 10, 11, 14, 15
Teen Vogue 26
Thorne, Robert 12, 24
To Grandmother's House We Go 12
TV movies 12, 14
TV series 16
tweens 6, 7, 26
twins 11
Two of a Kind 16
videos 14, 15, 16, 17
You're Invited to Mary-Kate & Ashley's 16, 17

About the Author

Jacqueline Laks Gorman has been a writer and editor for more than twenty-five years. She grew up in New York City and attended Barnard College and Columbia University, where she received a master's degree in American history. She has worked on many kinds of books and has written several series for children and young adults. She now lives in DeKalb, Illinois, with her husband, David, and children, Colin and Caitlin.